LEADER'S

GROWING
with the
ENNEAGRAM

GUIDING ALL TYPES
IN SPIRITUAL GROWTH

ELISABETH BENNETT

WHITAKER
HOUSE

Introduction images created by Katherine Waddell.
Photo of Elisabeth Bennett by Jena Stagner of One Beautiful Life Photography.

GROWING WITH THE ENNEAGRAM
Guiding All Types in Spiritual Growth

www.elisabethbennettenneagram.com
Instagram: @enneagram.life
Facebook.com/enneagramlife

ISBN: 978-1-64123-747-5
eBook ISBN: 978-1-64123-748-2
Printed in the United States of America
© 2021 by Elisabeth Bennett

Whitaker House
1030 Hunt Valley Circle
New Kensington, PA 15068
www.whitakerhouse.com

Library of Congress Control Number: 2021943181

1 2 3 4 5 6 7 8 9 10 11 **WH** 28 27 26 25 24 23 22 21

CONTENTS

WEEKLY PROGRAM GUIDE

ENNEAGRAM LIFE TYPE ASSESSMENT

PARTICIPANT CHART

*List of who is going through which
Growing as an Enneagram book:*

The Perfectionist:

_____
_____
_____
_____

The Helper:

_____
_____
_____
_____

The Achiever:

_____
_____
_____
_____

The Individualist:

_____
_____
_____
_____

The Thinker:

_____
_____
_____
_____

The Guardian:

_____
_____
_____
_____

The Enthusiast:

_____
_____
_____
_____

The Challenger:

_____
_____
_____
_____

The Peacemaker:

_____
_____
_____
_____

INTRODUCTION

Iron sharpens iron, and one man sharpens another.
(Proverbs 27:17)

THE LOGISTICS OF AN ENNEAGRAM DEVOTIONAL STUDY GROUP

You have the option to hold:

+ *An eight-week group*, with everyone reading two daily devotionals five days a week, and meeting once a week.

+ *A sixteen-week group*, with everyone reading one devotional per day five days a week, and meeting every other week.

You, as the leader of this group, will have this study guide as well as your own personal devotional. Everyone in your group would be buying their own individual devotional.

We have video teaching resources on YouTube for you to use at the beginning of each group meeting. You can find these on the "Enneagram Life Coaching" YouTube channel:

www.youtube.com/channel/UCgKdJ0j0Cg176qBoQg-rHCQ

The first week's video training would help each participant identify what their core type is and ultimately guide them to which devotional they should go through. This week can be skipped if everyone already knows their number. Each group meeting would start off with watching the video teaching together, then the leader will facilitate deeper application through questions and activities provided in this study guide.

Leader notes for each week are included for deeper understanding of each topic and guidance for the leader as they tie all nine devotionals together.

Whether you've led dozens of groups before, or this is your first time, we hope this guide and the training videos on YouTube will make this process feel easy and beneficial to everyone involved.

WHY GO THROUGH ENNEAGRAM DEVOTIONALS AS A GROUP?

"No one exists in a vacuum" is a common idiom that means you do not live unaffected by outside events and people, and what you say or do has an impact on those around you.

We live in communities, we are born to families, we are built for friendships, and we long for love. None of these building blocks of humanity are clearer than when we try to go without them. When there is no community there to help you, when you don't have a family, when friendships break, and when you feel unloved, life is hard.

In Genesis, we see that God made us to need each other.

> Then the LORD God said, "It is not good that the man should be alone." (Genesis 2:18)

This verse is commonly used in the context of marriage, but we also see the negative impact of being alone in any context where people are without community, feel unloved, or go without the simple human touch of another for long periods of time.

Proverbs 27:17 says we are like iron, and when we are living in community, we can't help but sharpen each other. We encourage each other, support each other, challenge each other, and help each other realize that there are realities and viewpoints besides our own. We become more effective in our everyday life when we are sharpened by God-given community.

As you embark on a study of our *60-Day Enneagram Devotional* series in a group context, I want you to know that this need for us to learn and grow together as a community is the impetus behind this program. It's fun to learn about your own personality, and there is definitely a place for that, but it is crucial for us to listen to each other, grow in our understanding of each other, and extend grace for those occasions when we did not realize it was needed before.

Community and relationship are one of the foundations upon which we experience God tangibly in our lives. We live as the hands and feet of Christ toward each other, and He uses us to enact growth and change in each other's lives.

THE DEVOTIONALS

The nine devotionals that we suggest for the participants in your group are:

1. *The Perfectionist: Growing as an Enneagram 1*

2. *The Helper: Growing as an Enneagram 2*

3. *The Achiever: Growing as an Enneagram 3*

4. *The Individualist: Growing as an Enneagram 4*

5. *The Thinker: Growing as an Enneagram 5*

6. *The Guardian: Growing as an Enneagram 6*

7. *The Enthusiast: Growing as an Enneagram 7*

8. *The Challenger: Growing as an Enneagram 8*

9. *The Peacemaker: Growing as an Enneagram 9*

Each devotional follows the same format, which includes the following:

+ Introduction: What Is the Enneagram?

+ What Does It Mean to Be (Your Type)?

+ All About Being (Your Type)

+ So I'm (Your Type). What Now?

+ Ten Daily Devotions on How You Reflect God

+ Ten Daily Devotions Dealing with Your Deadly Sin

+ Ten Daily Devotions on a Strength of Your Type

+ Ten Daily Devotions on a Pain Point of Your Type

+ Ten Daily Devotions on What Your Type Does in Stress

+ Ten Daily Devotions on What Your Type Needs to Grow

Figuring out your Enneagram type shouldn't be a one-time nt. Finding your type with accuracy is a journey that can people years. When we are introducing people to the and these devotionals, we don't want to pressure them or tell them, "You need to find your type right now!" We want to offer them this tool in an open way.

NO-PRESSURE DEVOTIONAL SELECTION

You might know everyone in your group, or they might all be people who are new to you. In either case, you may find these two types of participants:

+ "Mary" has never heard of the Enneagram before, but upon coming to your group and hearing about type Seven, the Enthusiast, she knows that's her personality type. She's super excited to buy the Enthusiast devotional and get started.

+ "Tim," on the other hand, has been studying the Enneagram for some time and still has no idea which type he is. He sees a bit of himself in every type, and picking just one devotional to go through feels like a lot of pressure. He thinks this group might not be for him.

Mary will feel easy to work with, and her excitement is what you probably envisioned when you thought of doing this group study. However, Tim might throw you for a loop. What now?

IF SOMEONE DOESN'T KNOW THEIR TYPE

If someone cannot narrow down their Enneagram type to one number, don't worry! Although these devotionals are geared toward one specific personality type, each day is based on Scripture, so any Christian could benefit from any devotional book. Each Enneagram type also has something in common wit' every other type, so no matter if they pick the devotional for their core number or not, they will probably have an *aha* moment about their personality.

As the leader of this group, your job is not to type everyone. Please read that again because I can't stress it enough. Enneagram types are based on motivation. Since we can only see *behaviors*, not the causes or motivations for them, it is unlikely that you will type members of your group with accuracy. What's even worse is that you could end up hurting someone who sees their Enneagram type, or the one you suggest to them, as the *worst* type. Obviously, there is no *worst* type, but many of us struggle thinking otherwise.

Be open, be kind, and let God open your community's eyes to reveal to them what their personality is. I find so often that people will mistype for years because they weren't ready to *really* know the truth about themselves. Only God should reveal that to them, so please do not force a type onto anyone. *You will be a good leader if you let mistyping happen, and you let each individual carve their own path on this journey.*

If you have "Tim" in your group, the following lists will provide some no-pressure information for him to pick his devotional. Read through the list, and ask Tim to pay attention to a couple things God would like him to grow in during this next season.

1. Pick *The Perfectionist* if:

    » You struggle with criticizing and not forgiving yourself

       Rules are very important to you

          u need to learn to loosen up and have fun

2. Pick *The Helper* if:

   » You struggle with thinking that your needs are a burden

   » Relationships are everything to you

   » You need to work on self-care

3. Pick *The Achiever* if:

   » You struggle with believing you need to achieve to be loved

   » You care a lot about how you are perceived by others

   » You need to learn how to rest

4. Pick *The Individualist* if:

   » You struggle with feeling like an *outsider looking in*

   » Being known and understood makes you feel loved

   » You need some organization and discipline in your life

5. Pick *The Thinker* if:

   » You struggle with having low social energy

   » Learning about topics of interest is very fun for you

   » You need to learn how to assert yourself and pursue your passions

6. Pick *The Guardian* if:

   » You struggle with anxiety and fear

   » You're a very attentive and loyal friend

   » You need to learn to relax and slow down

7. Pick *The Enthusiast* if:

   » You struggle with "shiny object syndrome"

   » You thrive when you have something fun to look forward to

   » You need to grow in focus

8. Pick *The Challenger* if:

   » You consider yourself a strong person

   » You will not be controlled

   » You need to grow in vulnerability

9. Pick *The Peacemaker* if:

   » You tend to avoid conflict

   » The motivation for most of your choices is, "What will bring the most peace?"

   » You need to grow in boldness

If they relate to many of the topics for multiple books, have them select the book for which they relate to the most topics, or the one with the topics that they feel like they need to work on the most right now. For instance, if they struggle with avoiding conflict and feeling like an outsider, but feel like God wants them to work on not criticizing themselves right now and they get angry when they make mistakes, that would be *The Perfectionist, Growing as an Enneagram 1.*

In the long run, there is no wrong pick. Each devotional is designed to bring us closer to God, and He is big enough to use whatever devotional you choose to grow you, even if it's not for your specific personality type.

DEVOTIONAL SAMPLES

Each devotional purposely has a very different feel. We had the advantage of addressing a specific group of people, so the writing style, shift in focus, and flow reflects that personality type. I also recruited the help of people with different Enneagram types to write some of the devotional days. It was important to me for everyone to hear from someone of their own type; this leads to those "me too!" moments when people realize others have the same issues that they do. Also, I humbly acknowledge that I am limited by my own perspective as an Enneagram Four.

You are likely to be buying your own devotional, and I sincerely hope God uses it to convict and encourage you. However, since you're leading this group, I want to give you a taste of all nine devotionals so you can get the feeling for what each different type is reading.

THE PERFECTIONIST: GROWING AS AN ENNEAGRAM 1

DAY 18 • • • • • • • • • • •

Controlling Your Anger

But I discipline my body and keep it under control, lest after preaching to others I myself should be disqualified.
(1 Corinthians 9:27)

In general, Ones have a very self-controlled personality. You probably have a natural inclination toward discipline and order, and we all know that inner critic is hard at work keeping you in line. This is why self-control is considered to be one of the ways in which Ones reflect God.

However, there is a vulnerability in the armor of self-control for Ones. That vulnerability is anger or frustration.

What makes you frustrated, dear One? Is it a situation? A person? Is it someone or something over which you have no control?

Are there situations or people disrupting your peace? Are they disrespecting you? In order for your inner critic to not jump down your throat about your frustration, which you may notice it rarely does, you have to truly believe in your heart of hearts that you are justified in your frustration.

Frustration may not feel like something *you* need to work on for yourself. You may think that it's the world that has to stop frustrating you.

However, as we've discussed, this frustration can be misplaced anger—an anger that, in many ways, has named you as judge, jury, and executioner. Your inner critic will allow the frustration, but anything further would be wrong, which is why the frustration itself doesn't feel all that wrong. Your inner critic knows that frustration is the dam that is holding back the rushing tides of anger.

But what is that frustration showing about the state of your heart? Your frustration might be betraying your pride, your selfishness, or your anger more than you think it is.

Frustration might feel like a relief, but simmering frustration is not really processing anger the way it should. Your frustration may not be as harmless as you assume.

SHIFT IN FOCUS

What does self-control in your frustration look like for you?

Do you believe God can help you with your simmering frustration?

What are some things that help you when you're feeling frustrated?

THE HELPER: GROWING AS AN ENNEAGRAM 2

DAY 21 • • • • • • • • • • •

What Is Boldness?

Since we have such a hope, we are very bold.
(2 Corinthians 3:12)

Dear Two, would you call yourself bold?

When a friend is hurting, when there's a right thing to be done, when a meal is needed, when a host is required, when someone needs a hug, what do you do? You don't hesitate. That, my friend, is boldness.

You're no weak or timid Two. Nurturing isn't a quiet task. You are bold, you take charge, and you do what needs to be done. There is a fight in you, and the Enneagram acknowledges this about your personality, which I think is perfect and so needed.

Boldness says, "Here I am; use me!" (See Isaiah 6:8.) Boldness says, "If you need me, I'm there." Boldness says, "I love Jesus more than I love my comfort." Boldness says, "I'm the right person for this job."

There's a confidence in boldness, but more importantly, there's obedience. Obedience requires action, and boldness is all about action.

Now you are most definitely not perfect in your boldness, but that doesn't mean it's not a strength. Over these next nine days, we'll dive deeper into what it means for you to be bold, and how to use this strength for God's glory.

SHIFT IN FOCUS

How does seeing boldness in this devotional about your Enneagram number make you feel?

Spend some time digesting what was said here. Then, identify four emotions that come to mind as you read it:

_____

_____

_____

_____

THE ACHIEVER: GROWING AS AN ENNEAGRAM 3

DAY 35 • • • • • • • • • •

Too Busy to Stop

Come to me, all who labor and are heavy laden, and I will give you rest. Take my yoke upon you, and learn from me, for I am gentle and lowly in heart, and you will find rest for your souls. For my yoke is easy, and my burden is light.
(Matthew 11:28–30)

We all hit a wall eventually, but as a Three, you might run a little longer than the rest of us. Along with Sevens and Eights, you have much more energy at your disposal than many others. This is fortunate because being motivated by worth can mean your life looks like a perpetual hamster wheel. Once you've accomplished one thing, you're on to the next without so much as batting an eyelash. You thrive off productivity, future plans, and constantly accomplishing bigger and better things. This can make things like rest, silence, or vacation feel very hard to prioritize. The high of accomplishment is just too satisfying to set aside.

However, I've talked to Threes who are struggling with chronic fatigue; perhaps they are in the midst of chemo treatments, on bed rest, struggling with anemia, or raising very young children. These Threes find themselves forced to slow down in a way that's not only hard physically, but also causes them to struggle with their identity and worth. They think, *Who am I if I don't have the energy to run life at the pace that makes me feel valuable?*

Who am I with an empty calendar? Who am I when I'm the one needing help? And they may not have an answer.

Unfortunately, there are too many Threes in the world who don't rest adequately and are *forced* to rest by some kind of stress-related illness, all because they don't know who they are if they're not busy achieving their next goal.

Thankfully we know that no matter our state of busyness, or whether we're productive or not, our worth does not fluctuate in Christ. We can lose all of our ability to be productive, impressive, or busy and not lose an iota of value in the sight of God. This is one of the reasons why God calls us to rest, not only in His commandments about Sabbath but also in what Jesus says in today's verse from Matthew. He will give us rest when we come to Him.

SHIFT IN FOCUS

Take a moment to look up stress-related illnesses and how stress manifests in your body.

Write down any symptoms with which you're prone to struggle. Use these as a red-flag warning that you need to rest.

What do you struggle to prioritize most? For instance, it could be sleeping, drinking water, eating healthily, or taking a vacation.

What would going to God with this area of your life look like?

What does God's Word say about this particular topic you struggle with?

THE INDIVIDUALIST: GROWING AS AN ENNEAGRAM 4

DAY 5 • • • • • • • • • • • •

We Help Others See God Through His Creation

And I have given to all able men ability, that they may make all that I have commanded you.
(Exodus 31:6)

One of the coolest things about being a Four is how others appreciate our gifts. So many of the artistic industries, such as music, film, fashion, and photography, are dominated by type Fours. Our heartbeat is to create, reflecting our creative Creator. And create we do!

Of course, it's not just Fours who enjoy a sappy, dramatic, sad song every now and then. Nor are Fours the only ones who enjoy performing, painting, architecture, and literature. All people enjoy these things, and every other Enneagram number is enriched by what Fours add to the world.

Humankind is drawn to music, nature, and other arts because there is a heartbeat, something so alive, within these. We often mistake this heartbeat as belonging to the artist, but it really belongs to God. Even when art is not God-honoring, it still, in and of itself, reflects a God who shows us what true art looks like through His creation.

When we worship an artist, it often results in the artist becoming miserable under the weight of glory, which is something we were never designed to bear. However, when we humbly allow ourselves to be the conduit by which honor and glory flow straight to God, we can live in the peace of our true purpose.

As Fours, we are responsible for what we do with glory. You may not think your life is very glorious, but look closer. You may receive a small taste of glory with compliments, or your first sale on Etsy, or applause after you speak on a stage, or thousands of likes on social media. Wherever you are in your journey, dear Four, glory is knocking at your door. No matter how much more glorious others' lives seem, you have something special, and glory has been a part of your past and will remain a part of your future. Will you kill yourself under the weight of it or will you freely offer it up to your Creator?

SHIFT IN FOCUS

Can you identify an area in your life in which you feel like you're being crushed by expectations?

What would it look like to rest in the Lord, giving Him both the weight and the glory for your artistic gifts?

THE THINKER: GROWING AS AN ENNEAGRAM 5

DAY 7 • • • • • • • • • • •

Living as a Lifelong Student
By Jarrett Bradley

Whoever corrects a scoffer gets himself abuse, and he who reproves a wicked man incurs injury. Do not reprove a scoffer, or he will hate you; reprove a wise man, and he will love you. Give instruction to a wise man, and he will be still wiser; teach a righteous man, and he will increase in learning.
(Proverbs 9:7–9)

What does it look like to be someone who is perpetually teachable? Proverbs 9 speaks to us about both sides of the coin: one person who has become unteachable, and another who continues to learn. It is easy to look at the proverb and see the stupidity of becoming the "scoffer" and the wisdom in becoming the "wise man." However, we have the advantage of reading the text from afar. It is quite another thing to allow the words to enter our heart and judge us for who we are *and* who we are becoming. Will we choose the path of the scoffer, or will we choose the path of the wise person?

Our first question should naturally be, "Why in the heck would anyone *want* to become a scoffer when it's so obviously the wrong choice?" The answer—perhaps just as naturally—is that no one in the history of the planet has ever aspired to become a scoffer...and yet it has happened, and it can most certainly happen to us. Perhaps our real questions should be, "What is in the heart of our proverbial scoffer? And what drives the *wicked man* to reject correction?"

The misalignment in the heart of the scoffer is undoubtedly that the desire to be right has usurped the desire for truth. It has become more important to protect the ego than to learn what may need changing in the heart. This state creates a porcupine-like character: quills out, ready to retaliate, or—more likely—to come off as so abrasive that none dare approach (even in love) for fear of getting stabbed by mere proximity.

Fundamentally, this state of the heart is about pride and, for the Enneagram Five, it is usually pride in the form of competency, or being perceived as competent. It can be embarrassing to feel incompetent, but that embarrassment only extends as deep as we have placed our meaning and purpose in what we believe we know. When our own knowledge is where we find our meaning, we are sure to become prickly whenever something, or someone, threatens it. It is only through Christ that our inner scoffer can be axed.

Through the gospel, Jesus offers us freedom from the need to be seen as competent. We are already loved by God, and to internalize that truth gives us leave to become a wise person—the kind of person who can embrace insightful rebuke and become ever wiser. In the gospel, our identity no longer needs to be wrapped up in being right or being seen as intelligent. We could be as dumb as a stump and still be loved by the King.

SHIFT IN FOCUS

Can you think of a recent time when you were agitated by someone correcting you?

Regardless of whether the person was right or wrong—since the feeling of agitation is what concerns us—where do you think that feeling came from? What was stirred in your heart?

THE GUARDIAN: GROWING AS AN ENNEAGRAM 6

• • • • • • • • • • **DAY 39**

Anxiety and Feeling Judged

> *Brothers, if anyone is caught in any transgression, you who are spiritual should restore him in a spirit of gentleness. Keep watch on yourself, lest you too be tempted. Bear one another's burdens, and so fulfill the law of Christ.*
> (Galatians 6:1–2)

As we discussed yesterday, anxiety and mental illness can be misunderstood. We may not even realize that we have stigmas attached to these things until it's spelled out for us, but everyone who struggles with either has felt the judgment and misunderstanding that comes with them. Especially and unfortunately, this attitude may be experienced in faith communities.

When we intertwine the mind and the soul, we come out with a lot of rules about what control we should have over our mind. This produces a lot of shame for those with mental illness.

All of a sudden, your postpartum depression is said to be a faith issue instead of a hormonal one, and your general anxiety disorder is proof of your lack of faith instead of an affliction you bear while trusting God for healing. Mental illness is not just for the weak and unbelieving. It's a symptom of us living in a fallen world filled with sickness, strife, and death. This is not how our loving Creator wanted us to live.

Many well-meaning people will try to bolster your faith when you open up about the anxiety, fear, or worry you're feeling; in some situations, they're right to do so. A lot of anxiety can be attributed to us grasping for a control we were never meant to have, and not thinking rightly about how mighty and good our God is. This is not always the case, but if it is, our brothers and sisters in Christ are urged to help with *"a spirit of gentleness."*

As the verses from Galatians remind us, we are to bear one another's burdens. No judgment, no condemnation, and no *fixing*, just mutually and empathetically bearing a heavy load.

+ If you were called out in a way that was not gentle and loving, that was wrong.

+ If you brought a burden to someone who should've helped and didn't, that was wrong.

+ If someone calls you out gently and you take offense instead of repenting, that's wrong.

+ If you hide your burdens out of pride, that's also wrong.

There's such a delicate line between encouraging another in faith and gently admonishing them when they have transgressed. We have all felt this done poorly and have probably had trouble walking that fine line when trying to help someone. But there is hope that people do care about you; they may just be missing what the actual problem is. As you care for those around you, I hope you'll let gentleness be your defining quality.

SHIFT IN FOCUS

If you have felt the stigma of mental illness and it's caused shame, that is a lie from Satan that God wants to redeem. The devil says, "You are broken and worthless" because he is the father of lies and there is no truth in him. (See John 8:44.) God says, "You're my precious child and in Christ, you are whole."

Shame is not something that you should be feeling with regard to your anxiety. Conviction? Maybe. Hope? Yes! But there is no shame for those who are in Christ (see Romans 8:1), and if you are a believer, that includes you and this battle.

How have you been loved well in your struggles?

How can you help bear the burdens of those around you?

Who do you need to check in with?

THE ENTHUSIAST: GROWING AS AN ENNEAGRAM 7

DAY 32 • • • • • • • • • •

Why Do I Do This?
By Molly Wilcox

So also you have sorrow now, but I will see you again, and your hearts will rejoice, and no one will take your joy from you.
(John 16:22)

We are living in a time of both joy and sorrow, the promise of heaven and our current life on earth, the already and the *not yet*. We believe Jesus will return, bringing total restoration and full joy, yet our day-to-day existence can still hurt.

Life seems unfair when someone we love gets sick, we lose a job, or we're just dealing with daily disappointments. But we Sevens in particular also feel a deep sense of hope and joy for the future—and so we spin.

Spinning often comes so naturally to me that my negative emotions, hurt, and pain turn into hope for the future and a joyful response. I take disappointment and immediately begin to tell myself a powerful story of the joys ahead. Honestly, I don't want to live in the hurt for long, so I tell myself of the hopeful endings I can anticipate instead of being caught up in the heartbreaking tension of the unknown. At times, this is a good thing. I tell myself of the hope I see through the brokenness in the world and I feel joy despite my circumstances.

Sometimes, however, I need to press pause in the moment of disappointment and admit to myself and to God that there is a disappointment here. I need to acknowledge that it's okay to feel its full weight.

My relationship with God is only true and honest when I allow myself to feel all of my emotions and allow Him to enter in and heal the hurt.

Dear Seven, I want you to cope and I want you to move forward from your pain, but I also want you to know your Father's heart. He is right there with you. When you're hurting, feel His healing presence. Know the goodness of rejoicing on the other side of sorrow.

I'll be honest, spinning a negative situation immediately into something positive is an innate trait for Sevens. I'm quick to proclaim *the bright side* and often it's a strength. But don't miss an opportunity to let God into the darker moments too because in those moments, He is still present and He is still good.

SHIFT IN FOCUS

Look back on the past few weeks or months and think of a situation you immediately spun into a positive. Think about the emotions you felt—perhaps anger, hurt, disappointment, or shame. Where was God in that? How can you invite His presence into that space?

Do you see value in stillness when you experience negative emotions?

Ask the Holy Spirit to guide you in this area and highlight opportunities to grow closer to Him in the coming weeks.

THE CHALLENGER: GROWING AS AN ENNEAGRAM 8

DAY 20 • • • • • • • • • • •

Living Under God's Authority

*Everyone who goes on ahead and does not abide in the
teaching of Christ, does not have God. Whoever abides
in the teaching has both the Father and the Son.*
(2 John 1:9)

Living under authority might not come naturally to you as
an Eight. You've learned to trust yourself, but you distrust most
other people, having known those who are fickle, incompetent,
or selfish.

The idea of someone else deciding what you should do and
how you should do it can prompt a visceral reaction from you.
How about no!

You're most comfortable being by yourself, responsible
for only you, or leading the pack—and there's not much in
between.

The good news is that living under God's authority is very
different from living under human authority. The latter simply
cannot be pure, selfless, and righteous. But God can *only* be pure,
holy, righteous, and good.

God gives us rules not because He delights in controlling
us, but because, like a good Father, His intention is our good.
He sets up boundaries and tells us not to cross them because He

knows the consequences of us going off on our own. He wants us to prosper under His rules and live knowing we will never be betrayed by Him. He fully sees us and loves us.

God is not man, that he should lie, or a son of man, that he should change his mind. Has he said, and will he not do it? Or has he spoken, and will he not fulfill it?
(Numbers 23:19)

If you've experienced trauma and tragedy, it can be hard to think of God as good, but that's okay. As theologian Paul Tillich said, "Doubt is not the opposite of faith; it is an element of faith." You can have doubts and questions. God is big enough to walk with you through them. He's not bothered by your questions, your anger at Him, or your thoughts. But He does ask that if we profess to love Him, we walk in obedience.

If you love me, you will keep my commandments.
(John 14:15)

Why do you call me "Lord, Lord," and not do what I tell you?
(Luke 6:46)

Walking in obedience is just another way of saying "living under the authority of Christ." God must be the absolute authority over your life, or lust is just waiting to take you for a ride.

SHIFT IN FOCUS

If you would like to read about what obedience to God looks like, the book of James offers lots of practical examples.

The truth is, all of us are living under the authority of something, whether it's God, ourselves, or sin.

Do you struggle to accept God's authority in your life, or is this an area that has become easier for you?

THE PEACEMAKER: GROWING AS AN ENNEAGRAM 9

● ● ● ● ● ● ● ● ● ● ● **DAY 37**

Identifying My Own Desires
By Alison Bradley

Commit your way to the LORD; *trust in him, and he will act.*
(Psalm 37:5)

I think it can be hard for other Enneagram numbers to understand how much energy it takes just to know what I think and feel as a Nine. Understanding someone else's feelings or opinions is easy for a Nine. Understanding my *own* takes work; sometimes, it can take *a lot* of work if there are conflicts involved in the decision or desire.

Merging often happens quietly and instinctually for a Nine. You probably tend to do it without thinking when you're with someone. Because of how easily it can happen, it can be hard to know where you stop and someone else begins unless you're paying attention and know what to look for.

I think where merging goes south is when we start to believe the lie that understanding is the same as agreeing. Our superpower is to understand someone else, and we do so easily. But that doesn't mean we need to agree with them or think they're right.

I've found that time alone is essential for me in knowing myself, so that I can stay awake to myself when I'm with other people. As a mother with small children, I don't have much alone time, but I try to protect the pockets of time I do have—or ask for some if I don't feel like I have enough.

I try to use some of that time for checking in with myself.

I ask questions like:

How am I really feeling?

Is there anything that is bothering me?

What happened today, and how did it impact me?

What's on my heart today?

When can *you* ask yourself these things? In the car on the way home? As you lie in bed before falling asleep? Do you have quiet time in the morning? Whatever moment to yourself you can claim, I'd encourage you to make these questions a part of that time.

Beyond just checking in, I also try to revisit the things I want to be working toward and the people I want to love. When I'm not using merging well, I can easily just let life happen to me, deferring to others about what I'm doing. I may not be using my time toward the things that truly matter without creating space to reflect in this way.

SHIFT IN FOCUS

What are my goals for this week? This season? How am I moving toward them? What might need to change for me to make more progress? Do I need to ask for help to move toward my goals?

Who is the Lord asking me to give my time to in this season?

You can make a list of people whom you see the Lord asking you to love in this season. It may not necessarily be the same people you've been asked to love in a different season.

These kinds of questions can ground you. They can help you remember the things you care about and your own opinions when you're with other people. You won't be so quick to agree to something if you've privately named your priorities for this season with the Lord. It will be much harder for you to fall asleep to yourself when you've done the work to show up when you were alone.

If you don't have space right now to answer these kinds of questions, pull out your calendar and plan a time to be alone and reflect. After you've spent time with the Lord, naming your desires and hopes, spend some time in prayer, committing your way to the Lord.

WEEKLY PROGRAM GUIDE

WEEK 1: INTRODUCTION
(Can be skipped if everyone knows their Enneagram type)

Let the wise hear and increase in learning,
and the one who understands obtain guidance.
(Proverbs 1:5)

LEADER NOTES

This is the first week that everyone is meeting as a group, and it may also be the first real introduction to the Enneagram many people in your group have. The "Ask an Enneagram Coach" section will help you navigate some big questions that may come up.

Feel free to make this group meeting a party! You're starting a journey to get to know each other in a deep way, and that's something to celebrate. Have a dessert potluck, play games, have everyone prepare the funniest meme they could find to show the group—your only limit is your imagination.

For those who already know their Enneagram type, this week should be easy; for others, especially those who are new to the Enneagram, this week will be crucial for them to get a good foundation before jumping into the remainder of the group study.

TIP

Watch the training video ahead of time so you can foresee any questions that may come up and free yourself from having to concentrate on the video while it plays.

ACTIVITY

Have each member of your group fill out a name tag that includes three attributes they would use to describe themselves. After everyone has arrived, go around the room and have each person explain why they chose the words they did. If everyone knows each other, they can simply write down their attributes. Also, you can go around the room and ask them to mention some positive attributes that they know about the other participants.

Watch the training video together.

Print out the Enneagram Life Type Assessment pages in the resources section at the back of this study guide and have those who do not know their Enneagram type fill them out. This will give people a fairly good indication of their type.

The sixty-day *Growing as an Enneagram* devotional books are sold through many outlets, including Amazon, Barnes & Noble, Christianbook, Goodreads, Bookshop, and a variety of local book stores.

As the group leader, you can keep track of who is reading what devotional in the front of this study guide.

QUESTIONS FOR DISCUSSION

How did you first hear about the Enneagram?

For those who know their type, how did the typing process go for you? (That is, was it fast or slow, easy or hard, etc.)

LOOKING AHEAD

Close by looking forward to the coming week, when everyone will be receiving their devotionals and then reading the first sections, which are the chapters before getting into the actual devotional days.

What is everyone excited to learn?

PRAY

Either as the leader, or taking turns as a group, pray for each other's hearts as you lean into growth as a group.

● ● ● ● ● ● ● ● ● ●

WEEK 2: GETTING TO KNOW YOUR TYPE
(First section in the devotionals, before the daily readings)

But the LORD said to Samuel, "Do not look on his appearance or on the height of his stature, because I have rejected him.
For the LORD sees not as man sees: man looks on the outward appearance, but the LORD looks on the heart."
(1 Samuel 16:7)

LEADER NOTES

For this second meeting—or the first meeting if everyone knew their type—the participants will have read the beginning sections of their devotional. These cover:

+ Introduction: What Is The Enneagram?

+ What Does It Mean to Be Your Type?

+ All About Being Your Type

+ So I'm This Type. What Now?

If someone didn't know much about their type or the Enneagram, they should now have a thorough overview. We will be answering the questions:

+ How does personality form?

+ How does Enneagram help us grow?

+ What is sanctification?

+ Who is really the source of our growth?

The information contained in the sections entitled "Introduction: What Is the Enneagram?" and "So I'm a (Type). What Now?" will be almost identical in all nine books. Thus, as a group, you all have the same information on what the Enneagram is and how these devotionals are designed to help you grow.

However, everyone will also be reading about their individual type, and learning about it in depth. This is a great time for everyone to share their thoughts on what they have learned about their type.

TIP

My Instagram site @Enneagram.Life offers IGTV videos that cover such topics as "How to find your wing," "What are triads?" and "What are subtypes and how do I find mine?" These may be helpful to watch before everyone arrives.

ACTIVITY

Start the meeting by watching the training video together.

Depending on the size of your group, you may find that you do not have all nine Enneagram types represented. If this is the case, it will be beneficial for both you and those you are leading for you to reach out to others with the missing type to see if they'd be willing to answer a question a week for you to share with the group. This will help everyone to gain a fuller experience of all nine types throughout this study. If you personally don't know anyone with the type you are missing, you can connect with others through Facebook, Instagram, and other forms of social media. I've found that most people who have discovered the Enneagram are happy to share their thoughts with others.

QUESTIONS FOR DISCUSSION

What was one thing you learned about this type that you didn't know before?

How would knowing that information your entire life have helped you?

Do you know anyone who you think is your same type?

If you had to quickly sum up your type for the group, what would you say?

LOOKING AHEAD

Close by looking forward to next week, when everyone will be reading the first ten days of devotionals about how we reflect God. Each type reflects our Creator in this way:

1. Enneagram One (Perfectionist) – Goodness

2. Enneagram Two (Helper) – Helpfulness

3. Enneagram Three (Achiever) – Drive/Action

4. Enneagram Four (Individualist) – Love of Beauty/ Creativity

5. Enneagram Five (Thinker) – Knowledge

6. Enneagram Six (Guardian) – Loyalty

7. Enneagram Seven (Enthusiast) – Joy

8. Enneagram Eight (Challenger) – Strength

9. Enneagram Nine (Peacemaker) – Peace

PRAY

Either as the leader, or taking turns as a group, pray for each other's heart as you learn about how you reflect God in the coming week.

● ● ● ● ● ● ● ● ● ● ●

WEEK 3: HOW WE REFLECT GOD

(First ten days in devotionals)

Then God said, "Let us make man in our image, after our likeness. And let them have dominion over the fish of the sea and over the birds of the heavens and over the livestock and over all the earth and over every creeping thing that creeps on the earth." So God created man in his own image, in the image of God he created him; male and female he created them.

(Genesis 1:26–27)

LEADER NOTES

We are made *imago Dei*, in the image of God, and this separates us from the rest of creation. We have souls that reflect the very image of God.

God is so vast that one of us could not possibly reflect all of His character, so we see glimpses of this in different personality types. When we come together as the body of Christ, we are most effective because we then have a full balance of God's image working as one body.

For just as the body is one and has many members, and all the members of the body, though many, are one body, so it is with Christ. For in one Spirit we were all baptized into one body. (1 Corinthians 12:12–13)

One of the coolest gifts the Enneagram gives us is naming how we each reflect God. In a society where many of us struggle to come up with an answer when someone asks us what we're good at, it's encouraging and even relieving to have an outside source say, "This is what you're gifted in."

Here's what each type has been reading about:

1. *Goodness*: Ones reflect God's goodness with their longing to be good and do things right.

2. *Helpfulness*: Twos reflect God's helpfulness with how they naturally look out for others' needs.

3. *Drive*: Threes reflect God's action with their drive to do, change, and bring value to the world.

4. *Creativity*: Fours reflect God's creativity by using their gifts to bring glory to the ultimate Creator.

5. Knowledge: Fives reflect God's love of knowledge with their pursuit of knowledge and wisdom.

6. *Loyalty*: Sixes reflect God's loyalty with the way in which they hold to their word and deed with integrity.

7. *Joy*: Sevens reflect God's joy with how they find the good even in a very bad circumstance.

8. *Strength*: Eights reflect God's strength with their drive to protect others.

9. *Peacemaking*: Nines reflect God's love of peace by being peacemakers in their own lives.

We are made in the image of God, and His very character is on display through His creation *in us*. We each display an important part of Him that benefits others and brings glory to God.

The Enneagram categorizes these *reflections of God* by personality type, giving us a glimpse into how God purposefully designed us and the gifts we bring to our relationships.

This week is meant to be all about encouragement! Everyone should walk away from this meeting realizing a gift they have and a renewed sense of urgency to share that gift with the world. They should also feel encouraged by seeing the gifts of the people around them, a visible demonstration of how God is working in their lives through others. Different is not bad; different is needed!

ACTIVITY

Start the meeting by watching the training video together.

Encourage each other. Go around the room and name the ways you see the others reflect God. If speaking these encouragements feels too awkward, you can pass around a notepad with each person's name on the top of a different page. Under their name, write a way you see them reflect God, then pass the notepad on to the next person. Afterward, give each group member the page with their name on it.

QUESTIONS FOR DISCUSSION

(Pick at least three)

+ What's one way you've seen how you reflect God play out in your life?

+ Do you praise God for the gifts and talents He has given you?

+ Out of all of the ways you get to reflect God, which is your favorite?

+ What's a strength others have that enables you to see God's glory?

+ How can you encourage someone with very different gifts this week?

+ Do you often name the reflection of God you see in others? Why or why not?

+ How do you see the unique giftings of everyone in this group working together?

LOOKING AHEAD

Close by looking forward to next week, when the devotionals will address deadly sins.

Is everyone in the group familiar with which deadly sin is attached to their particular Enneagram number?

Why is it important to be aware of and name our sin proclivities?

How will today's encouragement help ground you as we head into a convicting week?

PRAY

Either as the leader, or taking turns as a group, thank God for everyone's specific giftings and how you can experience that part of God through His reflection in this group.

● ● ● ● ● ● ● ● ● ● ●

WEEK 4: DEADLY SINS

(Days 11–20 in devotionals)

*If you do well, will you not be accepted? And if you do not do well,
sin is crouching at the door. Its desire is contrary to you,
but you must rule over it.*
(Genesis 4:7)

LEADER NOTES

Although the wording or specific idea for the *seven deadly sins* is not in the Bible, a list of these sins has been used by Christians for ages. These seven sins, plus two extra to make nine, are paired with each Enneagram number to give us a better idea of the specific vice that may be tripping us up again and again.

These deadly sins are often blind spots to us, so their exposure leads to repentance and greater unity with Christ. This is the greatest benefit that learning about our Enneagram number can do for us.

During the past week, each type has been reading about:

1. *Anger*: Ones hide their anger, but it often comes to the surface as a boiling frustration.

2. *Pride*: Twos' pride shows up with how they help others but don't believe they need help themselves.

3. *Deceit*: Threes' deceit often looks like people-pleasing and lying by omission.

4. *Envy*: Fours feel that everyone else has something they don't, a happiness and wholeness that is out of their grasp.

5. *Greed*: Fives hoard their sparse energy and many other things to help them feel like they have enough.

6. *Fear*: Sixes want control so they can feel secure, and they fear losing that control.

7. *Gluttony*: Sevens indulge in gluttony when they use anything to excess.

8. *Lust*: Eights' lust is not sexual; rather, it's an intense energy or desire toward something that is not theirs or not theirs to do.

9. *Sloth*: Nines' sloth is more about numbing to the outside world than actual laziness.

This week's topic is more convicting than encouraging, and your meeting may not feel as upbeat or fun as it was last week. That's really okay! This week is important too.

Deadly sins often appear as potholes in our lives; we fall in them and struggle to climb out. We may not feel like we have the power to fill these potholes or the ability to avoid them, but we know that God, in His goodness, will always provide a way around them!

Being aware of these specific deadly sins in your life is *key* to foreseeing when they may pop up and looking for God's way instead.

No temptation has overtaken you that is not common to man. God is faithful, and he will not let you be tempted beyond your ability, but with the temptation he will also provide the way of escape, that you may be able to endure it. (1 Corinthians 10:13)

This week is not about shaming your group into changing, but about helping everyone have the awareness that will prompt change.

TIP

South Hills Corona offers an excellent video sermon series on the seven deadly sins entitled "SE7EN." You can find it anywhere you get your podcasts.

ACTIVITY

Start the meeting by watching the training video together.

As a group, assign an animated movie character or any other fictional character to represent each deadly sin. Do these characters seem to also represent the Enneagram type associated with that sin?

QUESTIONS FOR DISCUSSION

Did the deadly sin attached to your Enneagram number surprise you?

As you reflected on this sin and its effects, did God convict you in this area?

Others' sins are often louder to us than our own. How does knowing of others' specific struggles help you to have grace and understanding toward them?

LOOKING AHEAD

Close by looking forward to next week, when the devotionals will cover lesser-known strengths of each type. These include:

1. One – Grace
2. Two – Boldness
3. Three – Encouragement
4. Four – Space Saving
5. Five – Objectivity
6. Six – Courage
7. Seven – Long Suffering
8. Eight – Tenderness
9. Nine – Gut Feelings

PRAY

Either as the leader, or taking turns as a group, pray for God to make a clear way around these potholes and help everyone to grow in this area of their life.

• • • • • • • • • •

WEEK 5: STRENGTHS
(Days 21–30)

He gives power to the faint,
and to him who has no might he increases strength.
(Isaiah 40:29)

LEADER NOTES

Each Enneagram type has unique strengths, but in these devotionals, we talk about lesser-known strengths of each type. This gives everyone an opportunity to be encouraged in a strength that they may not normally claim as their own, or one that is not named by others often.

Here's what each type has been reading about:

1. *Grace*: Ones have to work hard to have grace for themselves and others, making them very familiar with this aspect of God.

2. *Boldness*: Twos don't mess around when they see someone who is in need. They boldly take action and say, "I'm here—send me!"

3. *Encouragement*: Threes' orientation toward success enables them to spot potential a mile away, making them natural encouragers.

4. *Space Saving*: Fours do not fear your intense emotion. When everyone else can't make space for you to

process and express your feelings, Fours will be there with space for you.

5. *Objectivity*: Fives can separate their feelings from their thoughts, an invaluable strength when you need someone to look at a situation objectively.

6. *Courage*: Sixes have to be courageous every day, which makes them experts on facing fears.

7. *Long Suffering*: Sevens often put their reactions on the back burner to help others process first. Sevens are patient in pain and joyful in hope.

8. *Tenderness*: Eights have a strong outer armor that is protecting a very tender heart.

9. *Gut Feelings*: Nines are part of the gut triad (which also includes Ones and Eights), and their gut instincts can help ground them in reality and take action when it's needed.

Each type might have experienced this strength as something to be ashamed of or ignore at one point or another, so it helps us to call out these attributes as strengths.

Ones and Sixes are diving into a strength that is actually a struggle for average to unhealthy people of their types, but an attribute that becomes beneficial as they mature. Please be aware that any Ones or Sixes in your group who are experiencing struggles in their life right now may feel more convicted by these days than encouraged. Try to reassure them that this skill may be hard for them now, but a great gift in this area is within their personalities' tool box.

Encouragement, space saving, objectivity, long suffering, and tenderness—the strengths of Threes, Fours, Fives, Sevens, and Eights, respectively—can be traits that other people tend to take advantage of. As a result, these types may feel like these strengths leave them vulnerable. Encourage them to see these strengths as gifts to be stewarded and used for God's glory, even if they require some bravery to do so.

Boldness and gut feelings are strengths that Twos and Nines are usually trained to ignore, as they make them more assertive than most people appreciate. You'll have to encourage these types to see these strengths as the gifts they are! God does not see them as *too much*.

TIP

The *Sleeping at Last* podcast by Ryan O'Neal has an episode on each Enneagram type that is encouraging and speaks of these strengths.

ACTIVITY

Start the meeting by watching the training video together.

This activity is designed to help people reflect on their strengths. In the center of your meeting place, set out random objects such as a light bulb, a pen, a book, a pocket mirror, a candy bar, a coffee cup, a tea bag, a ball, and anything else you can think of. Make sure there are more objects than the number of people in your group.

One by one, have everyone select an object that appeals to them, then ask, "What are the strengths of this object? What do you use it for?" (For example, a light bulb enables us to see when it's dark, and it conducts electricity.)

Once everyone has shared their thoughts, go back around the group and ask, "What are one or two strengths you share with this object?" (For example, "I can light up a room, and my ability to ask good questions helps people see clearer.")

This activity will lead to some laughs, but also get your group thinking about their strengths.

QUESTIONS FOR DISCUSSION

Do you feel like your particular strength is encouraged or misunderstood?

Have others ever taken advantage of your strengths?

What's a strength in others that you appreciate?

What's a strength in others that is hard for you to accept as good?

LOOKING AHEAD

Close by looking forward to next week, when you will go over pain points. Everyone in this group has probably had a pain point of theirs pointed out to them at one time or another. If there is pain there, encourage them to revisit that moment with God this week and let Him heal that wound.

PRAY

Either as the leader, or taking turns as a group, thank God for the strengths represented in this group.

● ● ● ● ● ● ● ● ● ● ●

WEEK 6: PAIN POINTS
(Days 31–40)

If we confess our sins, he is faithful and just to forgive us our sins and to cleanse us from all unrighteousness.
(1 John 1:9)

LEADER NOTES

Just as each Enneagram type has specific strengths, each has its weaknesses as well. It can be just as important to be as familiar with these as it is our strengths, if not more so. Weaknesses can lead to sin, but if we know that they exist, we have an opportunity to watch out for them and turn to God for help to avoid them.

Some types' pain points will be more culturally unacceptable than others, but don't let the "lesser issues" fool you. For example, being self-absorbed as a Four might bring you more judgment than being a people pleaser like a Two, but both are putting something before God and are both sin in His eyes.

Each type's specific pain point can act as kryptonite in their spiritual life as well as in their relationships, no matter how small or great it may seem to the rest of us.

Here's what each type has been reading about:

1. *Inner Critic*: The voice that holds Ones to a standard and can often berate them for mistakes.

2. *Manipulation*: How Twos were conditioned to ask for love…without having to ask.

3. *Success Orientation*: The Threes' hamster wheel that never stops.

4. *Self-Absorption*: How loud emotions can become the only thing that Fours can hear.

5. *Low Energy*: A not-so-easy-to-hide trait of Fives that others often take personally.

6. *Anxiety*: The Sixes' voice of *what if* that fuels caution, fear, and suspicion.

7. *Spinning*: A scapegoat of Sevens for pain and discomfort.

8. *Intimidation*: The wall that Eights hide their tenderness behind.

9. *Merging*: A coping mechanism that Nines use to avoid conflict.

As with week two, when we addressed deadly sins, this week's topic is more convicting than encouraging. During your group discussion, please make sure no one is giving in to the voice of shame. Instead, everyone needs to realize that they are receiving grace from God as they grow and change by His strength.

There is therefore now no condemnation for those who are in Christ Jesus.   (Romans 8:1)

Although it can be uncomfortable and hard to come face to face with the most distasteful parts of ourselves, this is the beginning of growth and brings with it a cause for celebration. When what was hidden comes to the light, it might look undefeatable, but its exposure is the only thing that will lead to its demise.

> *Therefore do not pronounce judgment before the time, before the Lord comes, who will bring to light the things now hidden in darkness and will disclose the purposes of the heart. Then each one will receive his commendation from God.*
>
> (1 Corinthians 4:5)

Satan will try to take conviction and make shame your identity, which only leads to self-loathing, inactivity, and more shame. The enemy of our souls will tell you:

- "Look how sinful you are!"
- "See? This is why no one loves you."
- "Look at what you've done!"
- "You don't deserve anything."

God wants to take conviction and use it to change you from the inside out. With His infinite love, He says, "You thought you needed this behavior to fill your need for (fill in the blank), but I'm here, and I fulfill that need in you. Take My hand, child, and return no more to this, for it will only bring you shame and separation from Me."

ACTIVITY

Start the meeting by watching the training video together.

Play one round of telephone Pictionary. One person starts by writing a common Enneagram phrase on a notepad. (For instance, "I have balanced wings," "Don't type your friends," or "I'm on my typing journey.")

Then pass the notepad to the next person in the circle, whose job it is to draw that phrase on the next page. The drawing is then passed on to the next person, who writes what they think the picture is describing on the third page. You repeat this until everyone has either drawn or guessed the phrase.

Revealing what the original phrase was and what it ended up being at the end is sure to result in laughter. Starting off on a lighter note with a game like this can help to break down some naturally put up walls before heading into heavier discussion.

QUESTIONS FOR DISCUSSION
(Pick at least three)

+ What was your favorite day or quote from your devotional this week?

+ If you are not this type, what did you learn about this type that surprised you?

+ Were your eyes opened to anything new about yourself this week?

+ What does your pain point promise you? (Comfort, control, success, etc.?)

+ What does it deliver instead? (Isolation, fear, bondage, etc.?)

- Were you aware of this specific pain point before reading these ten days?

- What is an action God is calling you toward this week?

LOOKING AHEAD

Close by looking forward to next week, when the topic will be seasons of stress.

Is everyone in the group familiar with which Enneagram number is their stress number?

Is anyone in this group someone else's stress number?

PRAY

Either as the leader, or taking turns as a group, pray for each other's specific goals this week and against the trap of shame.

● ● ● ● ● ● ● ● ● ●

WEEK 7: GOING TO ANOTHER TYPE IN STRESS
(Days 41–50)

As servants of God we commend ourselves in every way: by great endurance, in afflictions, hardships, calamities, beatings, imprisonments, riots, labors, sleepless nights, hunger; by purity, knowledge, patience, kindness, the Holy Spirit, genuine love; by truthful speech, and the power of God; with the weapons of righteousness for the right hand and for the left.
(2 Corinthians 6:4–7)

LEADER NOTES

We all go through seasons of stress in life, and picking up coping mechanisms helps us feel some sense of normalcy or control. These coping mechanisms can be specifically tied back to your Enneagram type, and each type has another one they go to in stress.

Our stress number is the Enneagram type whose worst attributes we pick up when we are in stress. Discovering these tendencies can help us identify a stress season as it's happening and give us tools to access more helpful coping mechanisms.

Here's what each type has been reading about:

1. *One goes to Four*: Becoming hopeless and overly emotional

2. *Two goes to Eight*: Becoming angry and hostile

3. *Three goes to Nine*: Becoming slothful and numbing

4. *Four goes to Two*: Becoming clingy and fixated on relational hurts

5. *Five goes to Seven*: Becoming scattered and struggling with gluttony

6. *Six goes to Three*: Becoming competitive and overworking

7. *Seven goes to One*: Becoming critical and having energy to clean

8. *Eight goes to Five*: Withdrawing and disappearing

9. *Nine goes to Six*: Becoming anxious and trying to control that which they fear

Everyone's devotional includes a version of this simple exercise to use when they notice the *red flag of stress* pop up in their life:

+ Is something stressing me out?

+ If so, is there an action I can take to relieve some stress? (Make that appointment, have a conversation, pay that bill?)

+ If there's no action I can take, how can I be kind to myself in this season?

+ What do I need?

ACTIVITY

Start the meeting by watching the training video together.

This is a time for quiet reflection. Ask everyone, "What were the three most prominent seasons of stress in your life? How can you see these behaviors at work during that time?" Give your group ten minutes to journal their answers; afterward, they can share these with the group if they feel inclined to do so.

QUESTIONS FOR DISCUSSION
(Pick at least three)

+ Are you currently in a stress season?

+ What's the coping mechanism that's the most tempting for you?

+ How does this coping mechanism play out practically for you?

+ Which of these coping mechanisms was a lightbulb moment for you?

+ What is causing this stress season, or what caused your last season of stress?

+ What does being kind to yourself look like in seasons of stress?

LOOKING AHEAD

Close by looking forward to next week, when the discussion will turn to seasons of growth.

Is everyone in the group familiar with which Enneagram type is their growth number?

Who do you know who may be your growth number?

PRAY

Either as the leader, or taking turns as a group, lay hands on those who are currently in a stress season and pray for God's protection and grace to be upon them in a tangible way.

• • • • • • • • • • •

WEEK 8: GOING TO ANOTHER TYPE IN GROWTH
(Days 51–60)

And other seeds fell into good soil and produced grain,
growing up and increasing and yielding thirtyfold and
sixtyfold and a hundredfold.
(Mark 4:8)

LEADER NOTES

In seasons of growth, it's easiest for us to access the positive qualities of our growth number. These seasons can be harder to pinpoint than seasons of stress, but they are just as important to identify and dig into.

Here's what each type has been reading about:

1. *One goes to Seven*: Becoming joyful, fun, and less critical

2. *Two goes to Four*: Becoming emotionally aware and experiencing self-care

3. *Three goes to Six*: Becoming loyal and team oriented

4. *Four goes to One*: Becoming disciplined and consistent

5. *Five goes to Eight*: Becoming passionate and assertive

6. *Six goes to Nine*: Becoming relaxed and slowing down

7. *Seven goes to Five*: Becoming focused and objective

8. *Eight goes to Two*: Becoming vulnerable and caring
9. *Nine goes to Three*: Becoming bold and claiming their space

The very last day for all types includes this shift in focus:

Here, we are going to use 1 Timothy 4:15 as a guideline for action:

Practice these things, immerse yourself in them, so that all may see your progress.

"Practice these things"

Every new thing you've ever done required practice. Take baby steps, but prioritize the things that help you grow. Don't be afraid to be in the mindset of practice.

"Immerse yourself in them"

What verse that we mentioned over the last ten days really stuck out to you? I would encourage you to memorize it, write it out, and place it somewhere you will see it often. Immerse yourself in the truth of your worth in Christ, and you'll find yourself slowly but surely believing it to be true.

"So that all may see your progress"

Pick a couple of people in your life to share your big or small victories with. Be bold and share them as something worth celebrating. Can the people in this group be some of your growth cheerleaders?

ACTIVITY

Start the meeting by watching the training video together.

Have everyone pair off as accountability partners. It may be helpful for people to partner with someone who is their Enneagram growth number. Accountability partners will focus on encouraging growth in each other, support each other, and remind each other to stay focused. They should also decide how they will contact each other and how often. For instance, Mark (a Three) and Levi (a Five) are accountability partners and will meet once a month as well as text once a week for the next six months.

QUESTIONS FOR DISCUSSION

Is there a season of growth from your past that you're still reaping the benefits of today?

How could digging into these growth behaviors help you when you're in a season of stress?

What is one growth behavior you read about in your devotional that you plan to prioritize?

What's one action you need to take to help you develop habits around these growth behaviors?

LOOKING AHEAD

This is the last meeting for this group! Use this time to encourage everyone and reinforce the plan for accountability as you focus on Christ together.

PRAY

Either as the leader, or taking turns as a group, pray that God will help you to remember what you have learned and give you what you need in order to grow.

ASK AN ENNEAGRAM COACH

During the course of this group, there are bound to be questions that come up that leave you stumped. No matter how proficient you are in the Enneagram, there is always more to learn. As an Enneagram coach, I am constantly thinking I've learned everything, only to be shocked at how much I don't know.

This section is designed to help you troubleshoot some common questions and bring clarity to some more confusing areas of the Enneagram.

WHAT IS THE ENNEAGRAM?

You may have those in your group who have never heard of the Enneagram before, so how do we explain this system to others? Here is a brief explanation; every *Growing as an Enneagram* devotional that I have written contains a longer explanation that members of your group will read once they get their books.

The Enneagram is an ancient personality typology for which no one really knows the origins.

It uses nine points within a circle—the word itself means "a drawing of nine"—to represent nine distinct personality types. The points are numbered simply to differentiate between them, with each point having no greater or less value than the others. The theory is that a person assumes one of these personalities in childhood as a reaction to discovering that the world is a scary, unkind place that's unlikely to accept their true self.

The nine types are identified by their numbers or by these names:

1. The Perfectionist
2. The Helper
3. The Achiever
4. The Individualist
5. The Thinker
6. The Guardian
7. The Enthusiast
8. The Challenger
9. The Peacemaker

How Do You Find Your Type?

Your Enneagram type is determined by your main motivation. Finding your type is a journey, as we are typically unaware of our motivations and instead focus on our behaviors. While some motivations *may* produce certain behaviors, this may not always be the case. Since most online tests focus on behavior, you are unlikely to get accurate results.

To find your Enneagram type, you need to start by learning about *all* nine Enneagram types and explore their motivations in contrast to your own behaviors and deeper motivations. You can ask for feedback from those around you, but most often, the more you learn, the clearer your core number shines through.

It's often the number whose description makes you feel the most *exposed* that is your true core type. Your core Enneagram number won't change, since it's solidified in childhood.

Here is a breakdown of each number's distinct motivation:

1. Integrity – Goodness
2. Love – Relationships
3. Worth – Self-Importance
4. Authenticity – Unique Identity
5. Competency – Objective Truth
6. Security – Guidance
7. Satisfaction – Freedom
8. Independence – Control
9. Peace – Equilibrium

WHAT MAKES THE ENNEAGRAM UNIQUE?

The Enneagram is unlike Myers-Briggs, StrengthsFinder, DiSC Assessments, or other typology systems. In addition to delving into your base personality characteristics, the Enneagram is fluid in that it reveals how you change when you're growing, stressed, secure, unhealthy, or healthy.

You are not the same person at twenty as you are at sixty. You're not the same person at your stressful workplace as you are when you're at home binge-watching your favorite TV show and eating ice cream. The Enneagram accounts for these inconsistencies and changes in your behavior and informs you of when and how those changes occur.

In this graph, each Enneagram number connects to two other numbers by arrows. The arrow pointed toward your number is your growth arrow; the arrow pointed away is your stress number. When your life leaves you with more room to breathe, you exhibit positive characteristics of your growth number; when you're stretched thin in seasons of stress, you exhibit the negative characteristics of your stress number.

This is one explanation for big shifts in personality over a lifetime.

Another point of difference between the Enneagram and other typology systems is *wings*. Your wings are the two numbers on either side of your core number, which add flavor to your personality type. Although your core number won't change—and your main motivation, sin proclivities, and personality will come from that core number—your wings can be very influential on your overall personality and how it presents itself.

How Do You Become Your Type?

Personality is a kind of shield we pick up and hide behind. It is functional, even protective at times, but altogether unnecessary because God made us in His image from the start. However, we cling to this personality like it's our key to survival, and nothing has proven us wrong so far. It's the only tool we've ever had, and the shield has scratches and dents to prove its worth.

The Enneagram talks about childhood wounds and how we pick up a particular shield as a reaction to these wounds. However, not all siblings have the same Enneagram type even though they heard the same wounding message or had the same harmful experiences growing up. This is because we are born with our own unique outlook on the world, and we filter everything through that outlook.

Trauma and abuse of any kind can definitely impact your choice of shield as well. If you think of all these nine shields as being a different color, perhaps you were born predisposed to be more likely to pick blue than red. However, in a moment of early trauma, you might have heard someone shouting, "Pick black! Black is the only option!" Thus, you chose black instead of blue, which would've been your own unique reaction to your life circumstances. It's hard to say how these things happen exactly, especially when trauma is involved. Are you who you are *despite* trauma or because of it? Only God knows, but there is healing and growth to be found either way.

We've all heard the phrase, "You can't teach an old dog new tricks." I'd like to propose that when referencing personality, it might be said, "The longer you use your personality, the harder it is to see its ineffectiveness." It's not impossible for an older person to drastically change for the better, but it will be harder for them to put down what has worked for them for so long. That's why, as we age, it can become harder to even see where our personality ends and our true self begins. Even if the unhealthy parts of our personality have been ineffective, they still seem to be the only things that have worked for us.

CAN YOUR CORE TYPE CHANGE?

There are two schools of thought when it comes to how you become your Enneagram type. One is that you are born your type; the other is that you pick up your type as a response to wounds in childhood. I personally believe it's a mixture of these. I believe you are born your type, and troubling experiences you had as a child either cement that type or they change it.

Either way, as an adult, your core type will not change. You can't return to your past and erase any words or actions that hurt you when you were young. You cannot change your core Enneagram number.

However, there are several reasons why we may *feel* like our personality changes, including:

+ A change in wings, the number on either side of your core type that adds flavor to your personality

+ A season of stress or growth

+ A subtype change

+ Growing in your type

- Regressing in your type
- Being influenced into behaviors of other types
- Shifts in culture
- God's changing work in your life

WHY DO WE NEED THE ENNEAGRAM?

You may be thinking, *Do we really need the Enneagram when we have the Holy Spirit and the Bible to guide us?* Yes, the Enneagram is a helpful tool, but only when it is used as such. The Enneagram cannot save you—only Jesus can do that. However, God made us all unique, and we all reflect Him in individual ways. Learning about these unique reflections can encourage us and point us toward our purposes. The Enneagram also reveals sin problems and blind spots, and discovering these can lead us to repentance and change before God.

WHY ARE SOME CHRISTIANS WORRIED ABOUT THE ENNEAGRAM?

With every new tool, idea, or system introduced into the Christian community, some group pops up to oppose it. The Enneagram is no exception.

This personality typing tool has been growing in popularity in recent years, and interest exploded after it went viral on Instagram in December 2018. It has been especially popular among Christians, leading to disapproving Internet posts by the Gospel Coalition and others, including a podcast episode by Sheologians.

Nearly everyone in the anti-Enneagram camp expresses concerns about its origins and its impact on Christians. The most popular claim seems to be that the Enneagram has occult origins and was in fact given to Óscar Ichazo by an archangel while Ichazo was under the influence of drugs.

As a Christian Enneagram coach who also hosts an Instagram page on the Enneagram, I have read, listened, prayed, read again, and prayed some more about this topic for *months*. I have not taken these accusations lightly, and I feel a very weighty responsibility to know what I'm actually teaching here.

That being said, I was frustrated by how the history of the Enneagram has so much conflicting information surrounding it. For every accusation that Ichazo experienced demon-possessed automatic writings, I find an article where he praised his own brilliance for coming up with the Enneagram using physiology and wisdom traditions as inspiration.

Adding to the confusion, no Enneagram teachers—who have studied this topic the most—mention automatic writing or spirit-influenced origins for the Enneagram in their books or other written materials. This is even true of non-Christian writers, who (one would think) would be more likely to point something like that out.

This is what the Enneagram Institute has to say about the history of the typology:

The Enneagram of Personality Types is a modern synthesis of a number of ancient wisdom traditions, but the person who originally put the system together was Oscar Ichazo. Ichazo was born in Bolivia and raised there and in Peru, but as a young man, moved to Buenos Aires, Argentina to learn from a school of inner work he had encountered. Thereafter, he journeyed in Asia gathering other knowledge before returning to South America to begin putting together a systematic approach to all he had learned. After many years of developing his ideas, he created the Arica School as a vehicle for transmitting the knowledge that he had received, teaching in Chile in the late 1960's and early 70's, before moving to the United States where he resided until his passing in 2020.[1]

Should We Use the Enneagram?

We need to be careful with what we hold as truth in this modern age. We live in an era when if you want something to be true, you can find that viewpoint somewhere on the Internet. I knew I didn't want the occult origins to be true; I would have loved to learn that the Enneagram was founded by Fred Rogers, Elisabeth Elliot, or some other wonderful Christian, to be honest. But I also knew that I wanted the truth above anything else.

That's why I'm frustrated. Even Wikipedia says, "The origins and history of many of the ideas and theories associated with the Enneagram of Personality are a matter of dispute..."

1. "The Traditional Enneagram, Overview," The Enneagram Institute, www.enneagraminstitute.com/the-traditional-enneagram.

There are so many myths hanging around the history of the Enneagram, I don't think the truth of its origins is something we will ever be able to claim with certainty.

So, does it have occult origins? Possibly. But maybe the bigger question here is, "Is it possible for us as Christians to use something corrupted by the world for the glory of God?" I would argue that the answer is yes.

To give you just one example why I believe this is so, study the history of our Christmas observances. The traditions we have today to celebrate God's greatest gift to the world, Jesus our Savior, are pagan in origin, including the Christmas tree, gift giving, candle lighting, singing, and decorating our homes.

I would like to argue that even if the Enneagram stems from the occult, God is bigger than the occult. I believe I worship a God who can take what man intends for evil and use it to bring glory to Himself. (See Genesis 50:20.) I've personally seen this happen with the Enneagram.

I once went to a church where the pastor mentioned that there are three categories for how we approach things of the world:

+ We *reject* (sin, evil, and things expressly forbidden in the Bible)

+ We *receive* (love, kindness, and the fruits of the Spirit)

+ We *redeem* (holidays, tools, exercise, and ideas)

Through my studies and own reflection, I can comfortably put the Enneagram into that last category.

Even if you are skeptical of the Enneagram, I don't think it should be lost on you that it has non-Christians talking about sin—not only talking about it, but realizing that they themselves are the biggest issue in their own life.

Of course, there are some Enneagram teachers who would say that *you* are also your own savior, but we as Christians know that Jesus is the only source of salvation.

> *Jesus said to him, "I am the way, and the truth, and the life. No one comes to the Father except through me."*
>
> (John 14:6)

I've been able to use this tool to both show non-Christians their need for Jesus and also help Christians live out of their new selves instead of being falsely chained to old patterns of behavior.

In an article for *Relevant* magazine, Katie Jo Ramsey writes:

> The Enneagram is a tool that can reveal the specific ways we are held captive to our self as well as the unique ways God intends for us to display his glory and love to the world. More than a simple label, the Enneagram is a guide to receiving the transforming presence of Christ in the exact places sin and wounds make us fall short of the glory of God.[2]

---

2. Katie Jo Ramsey, "How the Enneagram Can Point You to God," *Relevant*, February 8, 2019, www.relevantmagazine.com/faith/enneagram-makes-sanctification-specific.

How Do I Teach This Tool with Confidence, as a Christian?

Besides the fact that I have not felt conviction from using this tool—nor have any other Christian Enneagram coaches I know—I cling to the fact that I have actually seen gospel fruit and change come from my work teaching the Enneagram.

People are yearning for self-knowledge, and the Enneagram gives them that, but it also tells them that they are their own problem. What a perfect segue to lead them to the solution to that problem, our Savior, Jesus Christ! Obviously, there are many teachers who tell you how you can be your own savior, and the Enneagram has been misused in our fallen culture. However, there *are* a few teachers like me who are using this tool to point people to Jesus.

Beth McCord is a sister in Christ who has been studying and teaching the Enneagram for years, along with her husband Jeff, who is a pastor. This is what she says regarding the accusations surrounding the Enneagram's origins:

The Enneagram is simply a tool. Any tool can be used for good or evil depending on whose hands it is in. The origins of the Enneagram are not clear and to assume that just because some who are far from believers who used it makes it bad or evil is illogical.

For example, a gun is neither good nor evil. It just is a gun. But in the hands of a criminal and used to harm others, it is being used with evil intentions. But when a police officer uses a gun to save lives, it is being used for good.

The Enneagram is a neutral tool that brings clarity into why we think, feel, and behave in particular ways. It is like a flashlight that shows us our heart's intentions. It reveals if we are doing well or not.

When being used correctly from a gospel-centered approach, it helps us to know if our heart is aligned or misaligned with God's truth in any given moment or circumstance—not to condemn or shame us (Christ took care of that) but to help us to see our need for Christ all the more!

I CAN'T FIGURE OUT MY TYPE. WHAT NOW?

Enneagram typing can be a long and sometimes frustrating process. As a coach, I've had multiple conversations with people whose family and friends found their types right away, but they themselves have floundered. When someone can't figure out their type, it doesn't mean there's anything wrong with them. The Enneagram can be a complicated thing.

There are a few main reasons why you cannot determine your type:

You're "Too Healthy"

The most distinctive characteristics of each type can be found in average or unhealthy people, so Enneagram teachers tend to use those descriptions to explain different types. It would be hard to tell types apart if we explained them all as being "mature, kind, and self-aware." *If you are very healthy, you will possess most of the better traits of almost all of the types.* If this is the case, it can be helpful to reflect on who you were when you were in your early twenties and what your core motivation is.

You're a Countertype

Each Enneagram type has three subtypes based on relational instincts: self-preservation; social; and one-to-one. These are addressed at the beginning of each *Growing as an Enneagram* devotional. One of these instincts will be dominant for you, and this can change how you are perceived by yourself and others. For example, a self-preservation Four will hide their more negative emotions in order to make others feel comfortable. This is a countertype, since it's not how Fours are commonly portrayed.

You're Not Ready

Self-awareness can be a devastating thing. God tends to reveal to us where we need to grow one step at a time; otherwise, we would be paralyzed by just how horrible and sinful we are. I believe God can hide some truth about who you are from yourself until you're ready to really process it. If your Enneagram type feels out of reach, pray about it. Now might not be the time for you to dive into this system.

You're "Too Informed"

Just like going to a candle shop and smelling all the candles, if you spend too much time researching the Enneagram, you'll slowly be able to identify with every type, making it nearly impossible to figure out which one you truly are. As an Enneagram coach, I like to think of myself as a palate cleanser to help people distinguish the types more clearly.

All of these common issues can be very frustrating to work around and figure out which is contributing to your mistyping, but give yourself grace and time. Reflect on the patterns in your life and start asking yourself a lot of "why?" questions.

For this devotional group, pick the devotional that goes over the topics you need the most work or encouragement in right now.

WHAT IF I DON'T RELATE TO SOME OF THE THINGS WRITTEN ABOUT MY TYPE?

You won't relate to everything that is written or said about your type, and that is fine. We cannot account for gender, culture, what Enneagram types raised you, your life experiences, and everything else that makes you uniquely you.

In these devotionals, we are exploring what *most* people of your type do or relate to, or how they may react under different circumstances. If you don't relate to all of it, that's okay!

I THINK SOMEONE I KNOW IS MISTYPED. WHAT SHOULD I DO?

If you think someone is mistyped, don't tell them that! As I mentioned earlier, God often won't reveal truths to us about who we are until we're ready. There may be people in your life who need to believe they're a certain number because that fits in with the view they have of themselves. God will reveal the truth to them in due time.

You can:

+ Pray for them.

+ Be patient with them.

+ Answer any questions they might have...but don't pry.

+ Give them resources such as the book *The Road Back to You: An Enneagram Journey to Self-Discovery* by Ian Morgan Cron and Suzanne Stabile.

WHY SHOULDN'T WE TYPE OTHER PEOPLE?

When you start getting really into and excited about the Enneagram, it is only natural to want to type everyone around you. However, this is a big mistake because you can *never* know someone's internal motivations, which is the backbone of Enneagram typology.

All that you can see from the outside is someone's behaviors, even if the person is someone near and dear to you. Although your brother may look so stereotypically like a Seven that it's painful, he might in fact be a type Three whose view of success is being the funniest person in the room.

You can teach someone about the Enneagram and encourage them to do their own exploring and type finding, but *never* tell someone what you think their type is. At best, you might be mistyping people; at worst, you are probably hurting them by turning them away from the Enneagram and robbing them of a very rewarding journey.

SHOULD WE TYPE CHILDREN?

Please, please, please do not type your children or anyone else under age fifteen. You should not type anyone except yourself, but especially don't try to type a child.

All of the most credible Enneagram teachers will tell you that type cannot be clearly explored and cemented until early teen years. In addition, you cannot and should not type your children because:

- You only see their *behaviors*. Children under fifteen usually cannot clearly articulate their motivations enough for you to help them discover their Enneagram type.

- Children change *a lot* between ages twelve and fifteen. In my own experience, before age twelve, my parents probably would've typed me as an Eight. Nope! I'm a Four.

- Your child will one day be able to type themselves, and that journey of self-awareness is very rewarding, like saving up money and buying something yourself instead of someone giving you the money or buying it for you.

+ You only have a short amount of time to enjoy your relationship with your child when they are young. Both of you will gain more from an Enneagram discussion when they're adults who are able to tell you their type.

However, this does not mean that you can't use the Enneagram in parenting. I think you should—not by typing your children, but by giving them all nine of the lost childhood messages that each Enneagram type longs to hear:

1. You are good because you're in Christ.

2. You are wanted and your needs are seen by God.

3. You are loved for you and you have the freedom to be who God made you to be.

4. You are seen and loved for who you are; you're enough in Christ.

5. Your needs are not a problem; even Jesus had needs and He was without fault.

6. You are safe because God is with you.

7. You will be taken care of because God will not fail you.

8. You will not be betrayed by God and He will sustain you if others fail.

9. Your presence matters; God made you with value and purpose.

CAN WE TYPE ANIMALS?

Animals are not created in the image and likeness of God and, therefore, they do not reflect God. Animals cannot have an Enneagram type.

CAN WE TYPE CHARACTERS AND CELEBRITIES?

For the most part, typing characters can be harmless fun. Although no character will fit into an Enneagram type exactly, there are a lot of good examples of types throughout pop culture:

1. Mary Poppins

2. Samwise Gamgee (*The Lord of the Rings*)

3. Tom Haverford (*Parks and Recreation*)

4. Anne Shirley (*Anne of Green Gables*)

5. Sherlock Holmes

6. Elinor Dashwood (*Sense and Sensibility*)

7. Ferris Bueller

8. Wolverine (*X-Men*)

9. Walter Mitty

We do not try to type celebrities unless they have come forward with their typing, and many have done so. Celebrities have real motivations, real souls, and real public relations agents who usually make sure those first two factors don't become visible to the public. We respect real people by humbly acknowledging that there is no way we know them enough to guess their Enneagram type.

I'M STUCK BETWEEN TWO DIFFERENT TYPES. HELP!

The following statements look at key differences between types, which might help you determine which one you are.

One: Good despite how it's perceived

Two: Good because of how it is perceived

One: Focused on the task at hand

Three: Focused on the outcome

One: Consistent, rule following, rigid

Four: Inconsistent, enjoys freedom, fluid

One: Wants clear communication, lots of reassurance, and lots of communication

Five: Wants clear communication, independence, and limited communication

One: Wants to be right, so their conscience is clear

Six: Wants to be right, to have the security of acting on true information

One: Struggles to break the rules
Seven: Looks for where they can break the rules

One: Focused on doing it right
Eight: Focused on getting it done

One: Has big opinions
Nine: Struggles to know their own opinions

Two: I must be loved
Three: I must be seen as successful

Two: I must be seen as selfless and generous
Four: I must be understood and appreciated

Two: I need people to adore me!
Five: I'd appreciate if others respected my independence

Two: I am overly trusting
Six: It takes a lot of time for me to trust people

Two: I want to be the person everyone thanks

Seven: I want to be at the center of the fun

Two: I really care that others like me

Eight: If you're not important to me, I could care less if you like me

Two: I will aggressively try to meet your needs

Nine: I will passively merge with you and make you feel understood

Three: Emotions are messy and often unnecessary

Four: Emotions are important and unavoidable

Three: I have lots of social energy and love small talk

Five: I have low social energy and do not enjoy small talk

Three: I want to be the leader, or I'm good at leading

Six: I don't want to be the leader; let me be part of a team

Three: I want my choices to impress others

Seven: I want my choices to bring me fun and adventure

Three: I need people to like me

Eight: If you're not important to me, I could care less if you like me

Three: I make decisions quickly and efficiently

Nine: I struggle to make decisions and it can stress me out

Four: My emotions are very hard for me to ignore

Five: If my emotions aren't making sense logically, I ignore them

Four: I romanticize relationships and the future

Six: I am very realistic about people and the world

Four: Sadness is a strong emotion that needs to be honored by fully experiencing it

Seven: Let's look at the positive! I don't want to be a downer

Four: I struggle with taking things personally and I'm much more sensitive than I'd like people to believe

Eight: I'm strong enough to take whatever you throw at me. I respect people who don't tiptoe around feelings

Four: Knowing what I want feels like knowing who I am

Nine: It's not natural for me to immediately know what I want or to ask for it

Five: I like to be independent and left alone to do my work

Six: I want to work along others and be part of a team

Five: I have very low social energy and prefer to observe

Seven: I have high social energy and love to participate

Five: My natural state of being is to not get involved

Eight: My natural state of being is to always get involved

Five: I have strong opinions or no opinion at all

Nine: I struggle to know what my opinion is and default to *your* opinion

Six: I don't need much to be happy

Seven: I struggle to feel satisfied with what I have

Six: I need to be aware of my surroundings and take precautions

Eight: I don't worry about much; I can take whatever you throw at me

Six: I struggle to slow down and rest

Nine: Resting is one of my favorite hobbies

Seven: The future is going to be amazing and I can't wait

Eight: I need to make the future what I want it to be and it's going to take work

Seven: People often describe me as upbeat, fun, and energetic

Nine: People often describe me as quiet, kind, and easygoing

Eight: I am not afraid of conflict; I welcome the challenge

Nine: Conflict makes me very anxious and I hate it

ABOUT THE AUTHOR

Elisabeth Bennett first discovered the Enneagram in the summer of 2017 and immediately realized how life-changing this tool could be. She set out to absorb all she could about this ancient personality typology, including a twelve-week Enneagram Certification course taught by Beth McCord, who has studied the Enneagram for more than twenty-five years.

Elisabeth quickly started her own Enneagram Instagram account (@Enneagram.Life), which has grown to more than 71,000 followers. Since becoming a certified Enneagram coach, Elisabeth has conducted more than three hundred one-on-one coaching sessions focused on helping her clients find their type and apply the Enneagram to their lives for personal and spiritual growth. She has also conducted staff/team building sessions for businesses and high school students.

Elisabeth has lived in beautiful Washington State her entire life and now has the joy of raising her own children there with her husband, Peter.

To contact Elisabeth, please visit:

www.elisabethbennettenneagram.com

www.instagram.com/enneagram.life

Enneagram Life | Type Assessment

● ● ● ● ● ● ● ● ●

HOW DOES THE ENNEAGRAM WORK?

The Enneagram is an ancient personality typology that categorizes personalities into nine different types. Enneagram types are determined by your main motivation, not behaviors, but since our culture is so behavior focused, not many of us know what our true motivations are. This can make typing ourselves rather difficult, but with some digging and reflection the answer is there if you want to find it, as this can be a journey for some.

Each of us has one core personality type that does not change, although different factors and our own health or unhealth can certainly make it look like our personality changes. Therefore when completing this assessment try to think of your life and behavioral patterns as a whole (over your entire life) and not just the season you're in now. By following these self-assessment steps, you'll have a good idea of what your core type might be.

STEP 1

Circle the statements that resonate with you.

STEP 2

Circle the specific typing statements that resonate with you.

STEP 3

Solidify your type with further resources.

Enneagram Life | Type Assessment

● ● ● ● ● ● ● ● ●

STEP 1:
Circle the statements that resonate with you most in each category.

CATEGORY A

1. I have been called intimidating.

2. I want people to be blunt with me.

3. I don't tend to let negative emotions slow me down.

4. I'm future-focused.

5. I'm not easily discouraged.

6. I think I have more energy than other people.

7. When I get into something I'm hard to slow down.

8. I care about the outcome more than the process.

9. I struggle with fear of missing out.

If you resonated most with Category A statements, go to page 5 for Step 2.

Enneagram Life | Type Assessment

● ● ● ● ● ● ● ● ●

STEP 1:

Circle the statements that resonate with you most in each category.

CATEGORY B

1. I don't generally feel like people understand me.

2. My work/life balance is a high priority.

3. I feel like I have less social energy than most.

4. I'm more past-focused (filtering present situations through what happened before).

5. I like to work at my own pace.

6. I don't tend to think of work outside of work, unless there's conflict.

7. I feel like my personal boundaries have been crossed when more is expected of me than I was originally told.

8. I have been told that I'm quiet.

9. When people prove to me they aren't worth my time, I'm done.

If you resonated most with Category B statements, go to page 7 for Step 2.

Enneagram Life | Type Assessment

● ● ● ● ● ● ● ● ●

STEP 1:
*Circle the statements that resonate with you most
n each category.*

CATEGORY C

1. I consider myself to be teachable.

2. I tend to be focused on the present.

3. I want my work expectations to be clear.

4. I'm not easily distracted from the task at hand.

5. My boss being happy with my work is very important to me.

6. It's easy for me to find problems and come up with solutions.

7. Clear communication feels like respect to me.

8. It can be hard for me to correct people, but I will if it's for the greater good.

9. Helping people makes me feel purposeful.

*If you resonated most with Category C statements,
go to page 9 for Step 2.*

Enneagram Life | Type Assessment

• • • • • • • • •

STEP 2 | CATEGORY A
Circle the statements that resonate with you most from each type.

THREE: THE ACHIEVER
1. Socializing is not a problem for me.
2. I'm very success oriented.
3. I don't like losing even in small things.
4. I'd consider myself high-energy.
5. I care a lot about people's impression of me.
6. I'm drawn to successful people.
7. I could talk my way out of almost anything.
8. I love when I get noticed for my accomplishments.
9. I had to grow up fast.
10. It's hard for me to rest.

SEVEN: THE ENTHUSIAST
1. I love having something on the calendar to look forward to.
2. Negative emotions are not something I like to sit with.
3. When I'm stressed, I tend to organize and clean.
4. I like to keep my options open.

5. I'm optimistic to a fault.
6. I feel a lot of pressure to always be the "happy" one.
7. I struggle with impulse control.
8. I'm an expert on fun.
9. I think a lot about the future.
10. I don't like goodbyes.

EIGHT: THE CHALLENGER

1. Being independent is important to me.
2. I'm very protective of my people.
3. Justice is very important to me.
4. I'm not a person that's easy to control.
5. I care about people but not what they think of me.
6. Physical exercise is very important to me.
7. I'm a natural leader.
8. I get offended for others but am not easily offended for myself.
9. I'm very decisive.
10. I don't want to appear weak.

Continue to page 11 for Step 3.

Enneagram Life | Type Assessment

● ● ● ● ● ● ● ● ●

STEP 2 | CATEGORY B
*Circle the statements that resonate with you most
from each type.*

FOUR: THE INDIVIDUALIST
1. I want what I contribute to the world to be unique.
2. My emotions are internally very loud.
3. I'm a creative person.
4. I'm abnormally comfortable with sad music or stories.
5. I struggle with comparing myself to others.
6. I spent a lot of time daydreaming.
7. My expectations (especially for special dates) often leave me disappointed.
8. "You're just like..." is not a compliment to me.
9. I think sadness is an important emotion.
10. I long to feel understood.

FIVE: THE THINKER
1. I have several topics of interest that I know a lot about.
2. I normally don't struggle with being overtaken by my emotions.
3. Others have called me quiet.

● ● ● ● ● ● ● ● ●

4. I prefer observation over participation.

5. I want to know "why."

6. I have been known to socially withdraw.

7. I feel like I have less energy than most people.

8. I'm calm in a crisis.

9. I need time alone to process and figure things out.

10. I'm a very objective person.

NINE: THE PEACEMAKER

1. I am not a fan of conflict.

2. I'm a pretty easygoing person.

3. I have a hard time remembering what I actually want/
   like.

4. Inner stability and peace are high priorities for me.

5. I have been known to procrastinate.

6. I have had at least one angry outburst in my life that
   was very unlike me.

7. I don't like to make decisions on the spot.

8. Letting others choose is often easier for me.

9. Sleep/rest is important to me.

10. I don't need things to be about me.

Continue to page 11 for Step 3.

STEP 2 | CATEGORY C
*Circle the statements that resonate with you most
from each type.*

ONE: THE PERFECTIONIST

1. I like my world to have order.
2. I was a responsible child.
3. It's hard for me to forgive myself for mistakes.
4. I tend to get frustrated when others don't follow the rules.
5. I want to do things the right way.
6. I take my responsibilities seriously.
7. Others can be surprised at how fun I am when I let loose.
8. Justice is important to me.
9. Following the rules is important to me.
10. I can't thrive in chaos.

TWO: THE HELPER

1. Being helpful to others is very important to me.
2. I think about my relationships a lot.
3. I don't want to be a burden to others.

4. Being needed makes me feel purposeful.

5. I feel loved and respected when others ask for my advice.

6. I thrive when I feel appreciated.

7. Nurturing/protecting comes very naturally to me.

8. People showing me affection makes me very happy.

9. I'm very dutiful when it comes to my responsibilities.

10. I tend to overcommit.

SIX: THE GUARDIAN

1. I have a select few whom I'm very loyal to.

2. I'd consider myself a well-balanced person.

3. I don't feel the need to be a leader.

4. I like to get second and third opinions.

5. I was a pretty anxious child (especially around bedtime).

6. I often worry about my or others' safety.

7. I'm a great motivator.

8.   I struggle to relax.

9. I have a hard time making decisions quickly.

10. Feeling anxiety is fairly normal for me.

Continue to next page for Step 3.

STEP 3

Your likely core Enneagram type is indicated by the type with the most circled statements from Step 2.

Congratulations on taking your first step in finding your type!

To further confirm your type, go to enneagraminstitute.com to read a thorough description of that type. Or go to @enneagram. life on Instagram to learn more about the Enneagram and read more on your possible type.

If you are finding that you don't resonate much with any of the three types of your first category, repeat Step 2 for the other categories to see if you resonate with one of the other six types more.

Welcome to Our House!

We Have a Special Gift for You

It is our privilege and pleasure to share in your love of Christian books. We are committed to bringing you authors and books that feed, challenge, and enrich your faith.

To show our appreciation, we invite you to sign up to receive a specially selected **Reader Appreciation Gift**, with our compliments. Just go to the Web address at the bottom of this page.

God bless you as you seek a deeper walk with Him!

WE HAVE A GIFT FOR YOU. VISIT:

whpub.me/nonfictionthx

WHITAKER
HOUSE